The Rules

by Meish Goldish
illustrated by Jackie Urbanovic

Harcourt
SCHOOL PUBLISHERS

Copyright © by Harcourt, Inc.

All rights reserved. No part of this publication may be reproduced or transmitted in any form or by any means, electronic or mechanical, including photocopy, recording, or any information storage and retrieval system, without permission in writing from the publisher.

Requests for permission to make copies of any part of the work should be addressed to School Permissions and Copyrights, Harcourt, Inc., 6277 Sea Harbor Drive, Orlando, Florida 32887–6777. Fax: 407-345-2418.

HARCOURT and the Harcourt Logo are trademarks of Harcourt, Inc., registered in the United States of America and/or other jurisdictions.

Printed in Mexico

ISBN 10: 0-15-350272-X
ISBN 13: 978-0-15-350272-9

Ordering Options
ISBN 10: 0-15-349940-0 (Grade 5 ELL Collection)
ISBN 13: 978-0-15-349940-1 (Grade 5 ELL Collection)
ISBN-13: 0-15-357306-6 (package of 5)
ISBN-10: 978-0-15-357306-4 (package of 5)

If you have received these materials as examination copies free of charge, Harcourt School Publishers retains title to the materials and they may not be resold. Resale of examination copies is strictly prohibited and is illegal.

Possession of this publication in print format does not entitle users to convert this publication, or any portion of it, into electronic format.

2 3 4 5 6 7 8 9 10   126   12 11 10 09 08 07

Crack! My bat met the ball hard. The ball sailed far. I watched it as I ran. It bounced off the outfield wall.

I passed first base. Coach waved me on. I ran toward second base. I picked up speed on the way. I passed second base. Soon I was racing to third. I looked to the right. I tried to see the ball. Where was it? I couldn't tell.

I had almost reached third base. Coach stood there. He held his hands straight out. That was a signal. It told me to stop running.

I didn't stop. Don't ask me why. I just wanted to score a run. I wanted it so badly.

I passed third base. I ran toward home plate. Coach looked surprised. He yelled, "Come back!"

It was too late. I sped toward home plate. My legs were pumping. My heart was pounding. The crowd was cheering.

Suddenly, I saw the ball. It flew ahead of me. The catcher caught it. He waited for me at home plate. He reached forward with his glove and the ball. The catcher tagged me.

"Out!" the umpire cried. I stood and dusted myself off.

I began to walk away. Coach stopped me. "Alex!" he cried. "What was that all about? I told you to stop!"

I smiled. "I wanted to score," I said. "I took a chance. I almost made it."

Coach looked very angry now. "Wipe that smile off your face!" he said. "You didn't follow the rules. Always listen to the coach. Play as a team. Those are the rules!"

I looked at Coach. "Sorry," I said.

"I'm afraid being sorry isn't good enough," Coach said. "You're out of the game for now. Sit on the bench."

I couldn't believe it. I'd never been out of a game. I was the best player on the team. They couldn't win without me. Coach knew that. Still, he put Brett in my place. Brett is not a very good player. I sat on the bench. I felt angry.

I watched the game continue. Our team had been winning. Soon we were losing. I grew very unhappy. I wanted to be in the game.

I saw Coach nearby. I looked at him. He came over and sat next to me. "Do you want to say something?" he asked.

"I want to play," I said. "If I don't, we'll lose the game. It's just a fact."

Coach looked at me. "That's not what I want to hear, Alex," he said. Then he walked away.

What did he want to hear? I had said I wanted to play. What else did he need to know? Did he want to lose the game? Didn't Coach care?

I watched Brett bat for me. The pitcher threw three strikes in a row.

Brett struck out. I knew that would happen.

The game continued. Soon it was the last inning. Coach sat next to me. "Alex, how do you spell the word *team*?" he asked.

"*T-E-A-M*," I answered.

"That's right," Coach said. "There is no *I* in *team*. Everyone is part of the group. Everyone counts. No one is more important than the team. Everyone listens to the coach. Those are the rules. Do you understand?"

I nodded my head. "Good," Coach said. "Now let me hear you say them."

I repeated the rules. I knew the rules were right. I knew Coach was right. I asked, "May I play in the game now?"

Coach called over the rest of the team. "Who wants Alex back in?" he asked. Everyone raised a hand. I felt really good! "You're in the game, Alex," Coach said. "Now let's win this together!"

Our team was batting. We were behind by one run. The first two batters struck out. Then Jake got a hit. Now I was at bat. I wanted a home run badly. It would win the game.

Crack! I swung hard. The ball flew far into the outfield. I watched the ball as I ran. The ball hit the ground and rolled to the wall. Jake scored easily. The game was tied!

Coach waved me on to second base. I got there quickly. I looked at Coach. He waved me on to third base. I got there even faster.

I knew I could get to home plate and score a home run. We would win the game! Suddenly, Coach threw out his arms. That was the signal to stop. I was shocked. I couldn't believe it. I could have scored!

I stopped at third base. Then, I saw the ball. The catcher had it! Coach was right. I couldn't have scored.

Juan had hurt his arm in the inning before. Brett now became the batter. I yelled, "Come on, Brett! You can do it!"

He did, too. Brett smacked the ball into the outfield. I scored. We won the game. We played as a team. That's a rule I can live with.

Scaffolded Language Development

PAST PARTICIPLES Review the following sentence from the story:

> The ball sailed far. *(page 3)*

Explain that *sailed* is the past tense of the regular verb *to sail*. Remind students that the past tense of a regular verb is formed by adding *–ed* to the end of the simple form of the verb *(sail/sailed, watch/watched, pass/passed)*. Help students recall that sometimes a spelling change is required to add the *–ed* ending, as in *carried* and *stopped*.

Reread the story with students and have them look for regular verbs whose past tenses are formed by adding *–ed*. Make a list of the verbs and their past tenses.

🍎 Health

Favorite Sport Have each student pick his or her favorite sport and brainstorm ways that playing that sport could improve one's health. Then make a list of everyone's favorite sports and their health benefits.

School-Home Connection

Play Sports Tell students to ask a family member to go out and do a sport with them, such as shooting baskets, playing catch, or going for a walk.

Word Count: 822